ORDER OF CONT[ENTS]

HOME DETAILS
PAINT LOG
HOUSEHOLD EXPENSE TRACKER
MONTHLY PROGRESS OVERVIEW
MAJOR APPLIANCE INFORMATION & WARRANTY
KITCHEN
DINING ROOM
LIVING ROOM
BEDROOM 1
BEDROOM 2
BEDROOM 3
BEDROOM 4
BATHROOM 1
BATHROOM 2
BATHROOM 3
ENTRANCE/HALLWAY
GARDEN
CUSTOM ROOMS

RENOVATIONS CAN BE EXTREMELY STRESSFUL.

IT CAN FEEL LIKE YOU HAVE A MILLION DIFFERENT DECISIONS TO MAKE AND THOUSANDS OF THINGS TO REMEMBER.

WHEN I RENOVATED MY VICTORIAN HOME, I WISH I HAD SOMETHING LIKE THIS.

I HAD HUNDREDS OF RECEIPTS FOR BUILDING MATERIALS/TOOLS/DECOR PURCHASES SCATTERED EVERYWHERE, I WASN'T SURE HOW MUCH I SPENT ON EACH ROOM,
I WAS CONSTANTLY CHANGING MY MIND ON ROOM COLOURS AND THEMES I LIKED, AND COULD NEVER REMEMBER THE NAME OF THE INSTAGRAM ACCOUNT WHO HAD THAT AMAZING MODERN KITCHEN.

SO I DESIGNED THIS PLANNER TO MAKE YOUR LIFE A LITTLE BIT EASIER, SO THE NEXT TIME YOU ARE SCROLLING THROUGH PINTEREST OR INSTAGRAM, YOU CAN JOT DOWN ALL OF YOUR IDEAS AND INSPIRATIONS IN ONE PLACE.

THERE ARE ALSO MANY OTHER USEFUL FEATURES THAT I HAVE ADDED.

I TRULY HOPE THIS BOOK HELPS YOU, WHETHER IT BE A FULL SCALE RENOVATION OR SIMPLE HOME IMPROVEMENTS OVER TIME.

GOOD LUCK.

HOME DETAILS

ADDRESS	
YEAR HOUSE WAS BUILT	
PURCHASE DATE	
PURCHASE PRICE	
MORTGAGE PROVIDER	
HOME INSURANCE PROVIDER	
HOME INSURANCE ACCOUNT NO.	

IMPORTANT CONTACT DETAILS	PHONE NUMBER

PAINT LOG

ROOM	BRAND	COLOUR	CODE	FINISH

HOUSEHOLD EXPENSE TRACKER

COST PER MONTH

BILL	COMPANY	YEAR 1	YEAR 2	YEAR 3

MONTHLY PROGRESS OVERVIEW

JANUARY	FEBRUARY	MARCH

APRIL	MAY	JUNE

JULY	AUGUST	SEPTEMBER

OCTOBER	NOVEMBER	DECEMBER

MAJOR APPLIANCES

APPLIANCE		SUPPLIER	
DATE PURCHASED		COST	
MODEL / SERIAL		DIMENSIONS	
WARRANTY INFO			

APPLIANCE		SUPPLIER	
DATE PURCHASED		COST	
MODEL / SERIAL		DIMENSIONS	
WARRANTY INFO			

APPLIANCE		SUPPLIER	
DATE PURCHASED		COST	
MODEL / SERIAL		DIMENSIONS	
WARRANTY INFO			

APPLIANCE		SUPPLIER	
DATE PURCHASED		COST	
MODEL / SERIAL		DIMENSIONS	
WARRANTY INFO			

APPLIANCE		SUPPLIER	
DATE PURCHASED		COST	
MODEL / SERIAL		DIMENSIONS	
WARRANTY INFO			

MAJOR APPLIANCES

APPLIANCE		SUPPLIER	
DATE PURCHASED		COST	
MODEL / SERIAL		DIMENSIONS	
WARRANTY INFO			

APPLIANCE		SUPPLIER	
DATE PURCHASED		COST	
MODEL / SERIAL		DIMENSIONS	
WARRANTY INFO			

APPLIANCE		SUPPLIER	
DATE PURCHASED		COST	
MODEL / SERIAL		DIMENSIONS	
WARRANTY INFO			

APPLIANCE		SUPPLIER	
DATE PURCHASED		COST	
MODEL / SERIAL		DIMENSIONS	
WARRANTY INFO			

APPLIANCE		SUPPLIER	
DATE PURCHASED		COST	
MODEL / SERIAL		DIMENSIONS	
WARRANTY INFO			

INTERIOR DESIGN PLANNER

KITCHEN

BUDGET: _____

IDEAS, STYLES & SKETCHES

INSPIRATION SITES & SOCIAL MEDIA ACCOUNTS

COLOURS

FURNITURE & DECOR

FLOORING

ROOM & FURNITURE LAYOUT

KITCHEN

DIMENSIONS:

TO DO CHECKLIST

KITCHEN

NOTES:

TRADESPERSON QUOTE COMPARISON

KITCHEN

DATE	COMPANY	SERVICE/JOB	THOUGHTS	PRICE

RENOVATION SUPPLIES LIST

KITCHEN

DATE	ITEM	SUPPLIER	COST
		TOTAL	

FURNITURE & DECOR PURCHASES

KITCHEN

DATE	ITEM	SUPPLIER	COST
		TOTAL	

INTERIOR DESIGN PLANNER

LIVING ROOM

BUDGET: _____

IDEAS, STYLES & SKETCHES

INSPIRATION SITES & SOCIAL MEDIA ACCOUNTS

COLOURS

FURNITURE & DECOR

FLOORING

ROOM & FURNITURE LAYOUT

LIVING ROOM

DIMENSIONS:

TO DO CHECKLIST

LIVING ROOM

NOTES:

TRADESPERSON QUOTE COMPARISON

LIVING ROOM

DATE	COMPANY	SERVICE/JOB	THOUGHTS	PRICE

RENOVATION SUPPLIES LIST

LIVING ROOM

DATE	ITEM	SUPPLIER	COST
		TOTAL	

FURNITURE & DECOR PURCHASES

LIVING ROOM

DATE	ITEM	SUPPLIER	COST
		TOTAL	

INTERIOR DESIGN PLANNER

DINING ROOM

BUDGET: _____

IDEAS, STYLES & SKETCHES

INSPIRATION SITES & SOCIAL MEDIA ACCOUNTS

COLOURS

FURNITURE & DECOR

FLOORING

ROOM & FURNITURE LAYOUT

DINING ROOM

DIMENSIONS:

TO DO CHECKLIST

DINING ROOM

NOTES:

TRADESPERSON QUOTE COMPARISON

DINING ROOM

DATE	COMPANY	SERVICE/JOB	THOUGHTS	PRICE

RENOVATION SUPPLIES LIST

DINING ROOM

DATE	ITEM	SUPPLIER	COST
		TOTAL	

FURNITURE & DECOR PURCHASES

DINING ROOM

DATE	ITEM	SUPPLIER	COST
		TOTAL	

INTERIOR DESIGN PLANNER

BEDROOM 1

BUDGET: _____

IDEAS, STYLES & SKETCHES

INSPIRATION SITES & SOCIAL MEDIA ACCOUNTS

COLOURS

FURNITURE & DECOR

FLOORING

ROOM & FURNITURE LAYOUT

BEDROOM 1

DIMENSIONS:

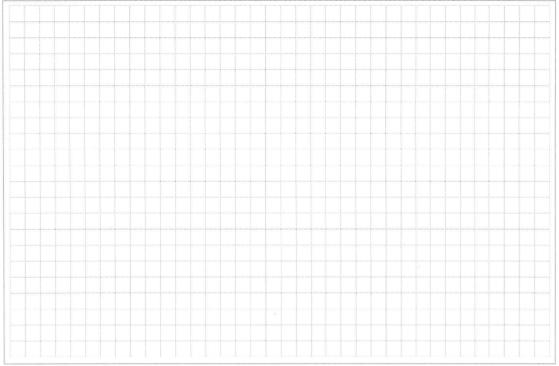

TO DO CHECKLIST

BEDROOM 1

NOTES:

TRADESPERSON QUOTE COMPARISON

BEDROOM 1

DATE	COMPANY	SERVICE/JOB	THOUGHTS	PRICE

RENOVATION SUPPLIES LIST

BEDROOM 1

DATE	ITEM	SUPPLIER	COST
		TOTAL	

FURNITURE & DECOR PURCHASES

BEDROOM 1

DATE	ITEM	SUPPLIER	COST
		TOTAL	

INTERIOR DESIGN PLANNER

BEDROOM 2

BUDGET:

IDEAS, STYLES & SKETCHES

INSPIRATION SITES & SOCIAL MEDIA ACCOUNTS

COLOURS

FURNITURE & DECOR

FLOORING

ROOM & FURNITURE LAYOUT

BEDROOM 2

DIMENSIONS:

TO DO CHECKLIST

BEDROOM 2

NOTES:

TRADESPERSON QUOTE COMPARISON

BEDROOM 2

DATE	COMPANY	SERVICE/JOB	THOUGHTS	PRICE

RENOVATION SUPPLIES LIST

BEDROOM 2

DATE	ITEM	SUPPLIER	COST
		TOTAL	

FURNITURE & DECOR PURCHASES

BEDROOM 2

DATE	ITEM	SUPPLIER	COST
		TOTAL	

INTERIOR DESIGN PLANNER

BEDROOM 3

BUDGET: _____

IDEAS, STYLES & SKETCHES

INSPIRATION SITES & SOCIAL MEDIA ACCOUNTS

COLOURS

FURNITURE & DECOR

FLOORING

ROOM & FURNITURE LAYOUT

BEDROOM 3

DIMENSIONS:

TO DO CHECKLIST

BEDROOM 3

NOTES:

TRADESPERSON QUOTE COMPARISON

BEDROOM 3

DATE	COMPANY	SERVICE/JOB	THOUGHTS	PRICE

RENOVATION SUPPLIES LIST

BEDROOM 3

DATE	ITEM	SUPPLIER	COST
		TOTAL	

FURNITURE & DECOR PURCHASES

BEDROOM 3

DATE	ITEM	SUPPLIER	COST
		TOTAL	

INTERIOR DESIGN PLANNER

BEDROOM 4

BUDGET: _____

IDEAS, STYLES & SKETCHES

INSPIRATION SITES & SOCIAL MEDIA ACCOUNTS

COLOURS

FURNITURE & DECOR

FLOORING

ROOM & FURNITURE LAYOUT

BEDROOM 4

DIMENSIONS: _____

TO DO CHECKLIST

BEDROOM 4

NOTES:

TRADESPERSON QUOTE COMPARISON

BEDROOM 4

DATE	COMPANY	SERVICE/JOB	THOUGHTS	PRICE

RENOVATION SUPPLIES LIST

BEDROOM 4

DATE	ITEM	SUPPLIER	COST
		TOTAL	

FURNITURE & DECOR PURCHASES

BEDROOM 4

DATE	ITEM	SUPPLIER	COST
		TOTAL	

INTERIOR DESIGN PLANNER

BATHROOM 1

BUDGET: _____

IDEAS, STYLES & SKETCHES

INSPIRATION SITES & SOCIAL MEDIA ACCOUNTS

COLOURS

FURNITURE & DECOR

FLOORING

ROOM & FURNITURE LAYOUT

BATHROOM 1

DIMENSIONS:

TO DO CHECKLIST

BATHROOM 1

NOTES:

TRADESPERSON QUOTE COMPARISON

BATHROOM 1

DATE	COMPANY	SERVICE/JOB	THOUGHTS	PRICE

RENOVATION SUPPLIES LIST

BATHROOM 1

DATE	ITEM	SUPPLIER	COST
		TOTAL	

FURNITURE & DECOR PURCHASES

BATHROOM 1

DATE	ITEM	SUPPLIER	COST
		TOTAL	

INTERIOR DESIGN PLANNER

BATHROOM 2

BUDGET: _____

IDEAS, STYLES & SKETCHES

INSPIRATION SITES & SOCIAL MEDIA ACCOUNTS

COLOURS

FURNITURE & DECOR

FLOORING

ROOM & FURNITURE LAYOUT

BATHROOM 2

DIMENSIONS:

TO DO CHECKLIST

BATHROOM 2

NOTES:

TRADESPERSON QUOTE COMPARISON

BATHROOM 2

DATE	COMPANY	SERVICE/JOB	THOUGHTS	PRICE

RENOVATION SUPPLIES LIST

BATHROOM 2

DATE	ITEM	SUPPLIER	COST
		TOTAL	

FURNITURE & DECOR PURCHASES

BATHROOM 2

DATE	ITEM	SUPPLIER	COST
		TOTAL	

INTERIOR DESIGN PLANNER

BATHROOM 3

BUDGET: _____

IDEAS, STYLES & SKETCHES

INSPIRATION SITES & SOCIAL MEDIA ACCOUNTS

COLOURS

FURNITURE & DECOR

FLOORING

ROOM & FURNITURE LAYOUT

BATHROOM 3

DIMENSIONS:

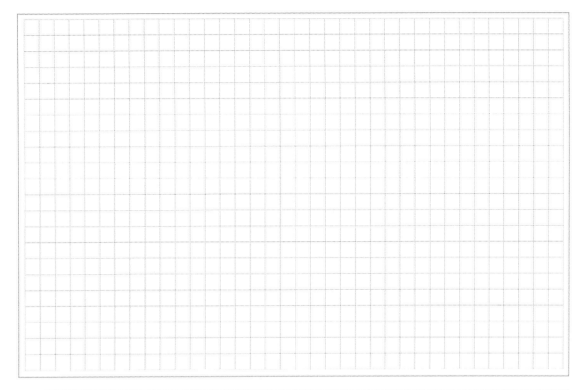

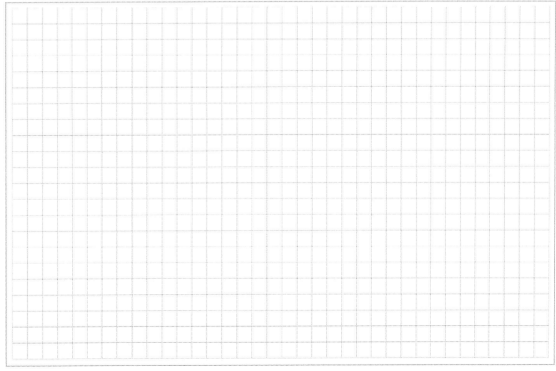

TO DO CHECKLIST

BATHROOM 3

NOTES:

TRADESPERSON QUOTE COMPARISON

BATHROOM 3

DATE	COMPANY	SERVICE/JOB	THOUGHTS	PRICE

RENOVATION SUPPLIES LIST

BATHROOM 3

DATE	ITEM	SUPPLIER	COST
		TOTAL	

FURNITURE & DECOR PURCHASES

BATHROOM 3

DATE	ITEM	SUPPLIER	COST
		TOTAL	

INTERIOR DESIGN PLANNER

ENTRANCE/HALLWAY

BUDGET: _____

IDEAS, STYLES & SKETCHES

INSPIRATION SITES & SOCIAL MEDIA ACCOUNTS

COLOURS

FURNITURE & DECOR

FLOORING

ROOM & FURNITURE LAYOUT

ENTRANCE/HALLWAY

DIMENSIONS:

TO DO CHECKLIST

ENTRANCE/HALLWAY

NOTES:

TRADESPERSON QUOTE COMPARISON

ENTRANCE/HALLWAY

DATE	COMPANY	SERVICE/JOB	THOUGHTS	PRICE

RENOVATION SUPPLIES LIST

ENTRANCE/HALLWAY

DATE	ITEM	SUPPLIER	COST
		TOTAL	

FURNITURE & DECOR PURCHASES

ENTRANCE/HALLWAY

DATE	ITEM	SUPPLIER	COST
		TOTAL	

LANDSCAPE DESIGN PLANNER

GARDEN

BUDGET:

IDEAS, STYLES & SKETCHES

INSPIRATION SITES & SOCIAL MEDIA ACCOUNTS

COLOURS

FURNITURE & DECOR

GROUND

DESIGN & FURNITURE LAYOUT

GARDEN

DIMENSIONS: _____

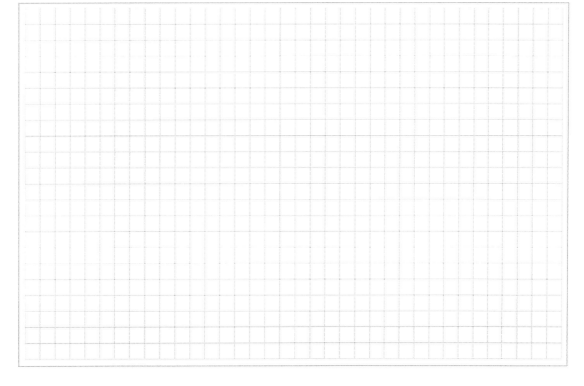

TO DO CHECKLIST

GARDEN

NOTES:

TRADESPERSON QUOTE COMPARISON

GARDEN

DATE	COMPANY	SERVICE/JOB	THOUGHTS	PRICE

RENOVATION SUPPLIES LIST

GARDEN

DATE	ITEM	SUPPLIER	COST
		TOTAL	

FURNITURE & DECOR PURCHASES

GARDEN

DATE	ITEM	SUPPLIER	COST
		TOTAL	

INTERIOR DESIGN PLANNER

BUDGET: _____

IDEAS, STYLES & SKETCHES

INSPIRATION SITES & SOCIAL MEDIA ACCOUNTS

COLOURS

FURNITURE & DECOR

FLOORING

ROOM & FURNITURE LAYOUT

DIMENSIONS:

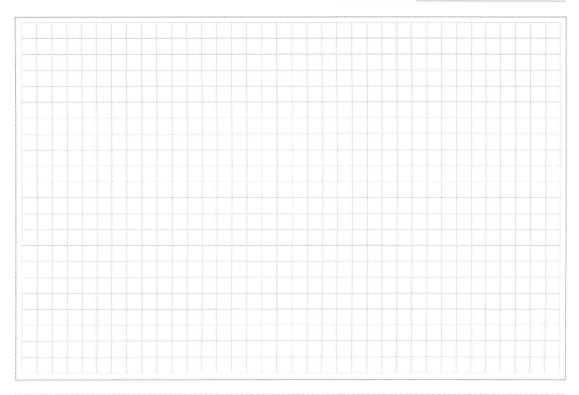

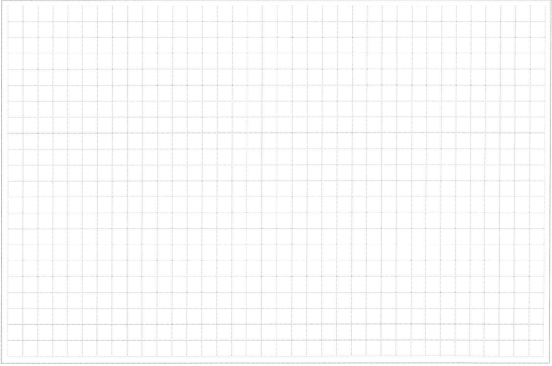

TO DO CHECKLIST

NOTES:

TRADESPERSON QUOTE COMPARISON

DATE	COMPANY	SERVICE/JOB	THOUGHTS	PRICE

RENOVATION SUPPLIES LIST

DATE	ITEM	SUPPLIER	COST
		TOTAL	

FURNITURE & DECOR PURCHASES

DATE	ITEM	SUPPLIER	COST
		TOTAL	

INTERIOR DESIGN PLANNER

BUDGET: _____

IDEAS, STYLES & SKETCHES

INSPIRATION SITES & SOCIAL MEDIA ACCOUNTS

COLOURS

FURNITURE & DECOR

FLOORING

ROOM & FURNITURE LAYOUT

DIMENSIONS:

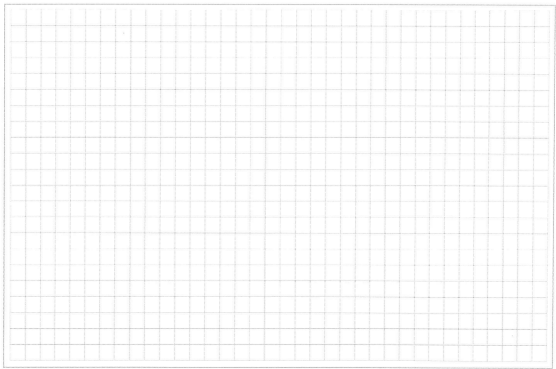

TO DO CHECKLIST

NOTES:

TRADESPERSON QUOTE COMPARISON

DATE	COMPANY	SERVICE/JOB	THOUGHTS	PRICE

RENOVATION SUPPLIES LIST

DATE	ITEM	SUPPLIER	COST
		TOTAL	

FURNITURE & DECOR PURCHASES

DATE	ITEM	SUPPLIER	COST
		TOTAL	

INTERIOR DESIGN PLANNER

BUDGET: _____

IDEAS, STYLES & SKETCHES

INSPIRATION SITES & SOCIAL MEDIA ACCOUNTS

COLOURS

FURNITURE & DECOR

FLOORING

ROOM & FURNITURE LAYOUT

DIMENSIONS: _____

TRADESPERSON QUOTE COMPARISON

DATE	COMPANY	SERVICE/JOB	THOUGHTS	PRICE

RENOVATION SUPPLIES LIST

DATE	ITEM	SUPPLIER	COST
		TOTAL	

FURNITURE & DECOR PURCHASES

DATE	ITEM	SUPPLIER	COST
		TOTAL	

INTERIOR DESIGN PLANNER

BUDGET: _____

IDEAS, STYLES & SKETCHES

INSPIRATION SITES & SOCIAL MEDIA ACCOUNTS

COLOURS

FURNITURE & DECOR

FLOORING

ROOM & FURNITURE LAYOUT

DIMENSIONS: _____

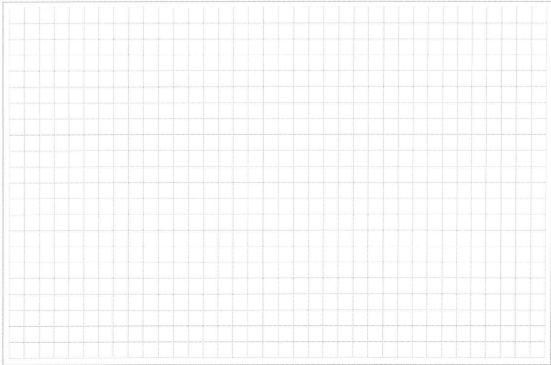

TO DO CHECKLIST

NOTES:

TRADESPERSON QUOTE COMPARISON

DATE	COMPANY	SERVICE/JOB	THOUGHTS	PRICE

RENOVATION SUPPLIES LIST

DATE	ITEM	SUPPLIER	COST
		TOTAL	

FURNITURE & DECOR PURCHASES

DATE	ITEM	SUPPLIER	COST
		TOTAL	

Made in the USA
Monee, IL
05 October 2024

67272149R00057